REFLEC
FOR I

CW00857706

REFLECTIONS
FOR
LENT

9 March – 23 April 2011

JEFF ASTLEY
CHRISTOPHER HERBERT
ANN LEWIN

Church House Publishing
Church House
Great Smith Street
London SW1P 3AZ

ISBN 978 0 7151 4231 8

Published 2010 by Church House Publishing
Copyright © The Archbishops' Council 2010

Designed and typeset by Hugh Hillyard-Parker
Printed by CPI Antony Rowe, Chippenham, Wiltshire

Contents

About the authors

Jeff Astley is Honorary Professorial Fellow in Practical Theology and Christian Education, University of Durham, and Director of the North of England Institute for Christian Education. He has worked in parish ministry, university chaplaincy and higher education and is the author of several books, including *Christ of the Everyday*.

Christopher Herbert was Bishop of St Albans from 1995 to 2009. He has an interest in, and love for, all forms of literature and is a prolific author in his own right. Much of his writing is based on the themes of prayer and spirituality, for both children and adults. Among his best-known books are *Ways into Prayer* and *Pocket Prayers*.

Ann Lewin was a secondary-school teacher for 27 years (RE and English) and ended her working life as a Welfare Adviser for International Students at Southampton University. She writes (e.g. *Watching for the Kingfisher*, published by Canterbury Press), and leads retreats and quiet days. Interests include reading, birdwatching, music, theatre and the company of friends.

About *Reflections for Lent*

Based on the *Common Worship Lectionary* readings for Morning Prayer, these daily reflections are is designed to enhance your spiritual journey though the forty days from Ash Wednesday to Holy Saturday. The aim is to provide rich, contemporary and engaging insights into Scripture, refreshing and inspiring times of personal prayer.

Each page lists the lectionary readings for the day, with the main psalms for that day highlighted in **bold**. The Collect of the day – either the *Common Worship* collect or the shorter additional collect – is also included.

For those using this book in conjunction with a service of Morning Prayer, the following conventions apply: a psalm printed in parentheses is omitted if it has been used as the opening canticle at that office; a psalm marked with an asterisk may be shortened if desired.

A short reflection is provided on either the Old or New Testament reading. The reflections have been written by three highly respected Christian authors, all bringing their own emphases, enthusiasms and approaches to biblical interpretation to bear.

Regular users of Morning Prayer and *Time to Pray* (from *Common Worship: Daily Prayer*) and anyone who follows the lectionary for their regular Bible reading will benefit from the rich variety of traditions represented in these stimulating and accessible pieces.

If you would like to continue the pattern of daily reading and reflection in this book beyond Lent, an annual volume of *Reflections for Daily Prayer* is also available. Please see the back page of this book for more details.

Psalm **38**
Daniel 9.3-6,17-19
1 Timothy 6.6-19

1 Timothy 6.6-19

'Fight the good fight of the faith' (v.12)

At the beginning of Lent, we read of temptation (v.9) and 'the good fight of the faith' (v.12 – the fight being an image from competitive athletics rather than warfare). Scholars have suggested that verses 11 to 16 come from a baptismal liturgy, or perhaps an ordination address.

Lent is a time for spiritual realism. The author follows Job in recognizing our intrinsic poverty (v.7, cf. Job 1.21). Lacking possessions, we come to crave them. Self-interest, famously presented here as the love of money, is one of those root sins that spiritually distract us from focusing on God, the only source of true riches (vv.10, 17). We then drown in spiritual self-destruction. There are references to the future (v.19). But, as in John's Gospel, 'eternal life' is presented as something that can be Timothy's *present* possession (v.12). This is true life, real life, life directed towards God. It is no transient thing; it must be fulfilled. But fighting the good fight is a matter of grasping hold of it *now*.

Part of this, key to the Lenten life, is a deeper sort of 'grasping': a matter of understanding – of seeing the point of – life. Spiritual realism knows that life is really about giving, not getting-and-holding (v.18) – as is the God of Jesus (v.13).

COLLECT

Almighty and everlasting God,
you hate nothing that you have made
and forgive the sins of all those who are penitent:
create and make in us new and contrite hearts
that we, worthily lamenting our sins
and acknowledging our wretchedness,
may receive from you, the God of all mercy,
perfect remission and forgiveness;
through Jesus Christ your Son our Lord,
who is alive and reigns with you,
in the unity of the Holy Spirit,
one God, now and for ever.

Psalms **77** *or* 113, **115**
Jeremiah 2.14-32
John 4.1-26

Jeremiah 2.14-32

'... my people have forgotten me' (v.32)

God seems puzzled. Israel's northern kingdom fell to Assyria in 722 BC. The southern kingdom of Judah, where Jeremiah prophesies, is now threatened by enemies. Why? Is it because of its lowly status (v.14)?

Yahweh, God alone, knows the real reason for their suffering: in breaking her marriage vows and abandoning her faithful partner (v.17), Israel has found only the freedom of the prey at the mercy of lions (v.15).

Freedom is often a two-edged sword. We yearn for it when restrained by parents, employers, spouses, life. But, although the freedom to choose is always good, it is the same freedom that allows us to embrace and create what is bad – for ourselves sometimes, often for others. It is not enough just to be free. It depends on what we are freeing ourselves from and freeing ourselves for, and how we use that freedom. Jeremiah paints a poignant picture of an unrestrained, degenerate freedom that becomes an indiscriminate, unfulfilling and 'hopeless' love of strangers (vv.20-25).

Yahweh laments his lost love, who turned her back on his faithfulness and refuses to give up her freedom and return home (v.31). Here is a God who *feels*, who can be *hurt*: a God who is vulnerable, and truly cares whether we still love him or not.

Holy God,
our lives are laid open before you:
rescue us from the chaos of sin
and through the death of your Son
bring us healing and make us whole
in Jesus Christ our Lord.

COLLECT

3

Friday 11 March

Jeremiah 3.6-22

'I thought you would call me, My Father' (v.19)

When spurned lovers or hurt parents confide in a trusted friend, talking of their betrayal, they will speak of pain and recrimination. But, if love is still alive in the damaged relationship, deeper feelings of affection and forgiveness will eventually tumble into expression.

Is God very different? We might expect that a just God, who can alone occupy the moral high ground without fear of slipping, would maintain his righteous indignation longer than we could. But not so. God is infinite in all things, but limitless love always trumps untrammelled justice. Ultimately, God's forgiveness can know no bounds. He *yearns* for us.

The northern kingdom, Israel, sinned first – and fell to the Assyrians. Southern Judah is going the same way – indeed, she is already further along it (vv.6-11). But Yahweh's faithfulness and love, as husband and father, will not allow him to 'be angry for ever'. He will bring whoever will come – from both Israel and Judah – back to Jerusalem (vv.14,18), despite their fickleness.

Few texts are as poignantly expressive of the character of God, and the hope implicit in the human response, than verses 19 to 22: I thought you would call me 'father', but you have turned, left and forgotten me. Come back ... Be healed ...

COLLECT

Almighty and everlasting God,
you hate nothing that you have made
and forgive the sins of all those who are penitent:
create and make in us new and contrite hearts
that we, worthily lamenting our sins
and acknowledging our wretchedness,
may receive from you, the God of all mercy,
perfect remission and forgiveness;
through Jesus Christ your Son our Lord,
who is alive and reigns with you,
in the unity of the Holy Spirit,
one God, now and for ever.

Psalms **71** *or* 120, **121**, 122
Jeremiah 4.1-18
John 4.43-end

Saturday 12 March

Jeremiah 4.1-18

'... a destroyer of nations has set out' (v.7)

The German Protestant theologian, Rudolf Otto, wrote of the experience of holiness as two-sided. The holy is entrancing, attractive. We speak of it – of him/her – as good. But there is dread and terror as well. Moses before the burning bush and the disciples witnessing the transfiguration were captivated and enthralled, but fearful too. Talk of judgement articulates this stormy side of God's love.

This is how it is: turning away from the light and warmth of grace, we stumble into the cold, dark side of holy fear. 'Do not be deceived ... you reap whatever you sow' (Galatians 6.7).

A stroppy, defiant adolescent might respond to a parent's demand by shouting 'Or else what ...?' Israel and Judah, by betraying God's love, now face the answer to that question.

So, the mood changes and the sky darkens. Turn your back on God, and you face what is not-God, and must face it alone. God's love is personal. His 'wrath', however, sounds like an impersonal, unavoidable force: the virulent consequence of human evil (v.4). The images pile up – the lion, the destroyer, the scorching from the desert, the whirlwind. In plain language: 'besiegers ... from a distant land' (v.16).

The enemies of Israel are come, because of her rebellion. 'This is your *doom*.'

COLLECT

Holy God,
our lives are laid open before you:
rescue us from the chaos of sin
and through the death of your Son
bring us healing and make us whole
in Jesus Christ our Lord.

5

Jeremiah 4.19-end

'The whole land shall be a desolation; yet ...' (v.27)

The prophet spells out in vivid, personal images what this disaster will mean to the 'stupid children' of Israel. It means the destruction of tents (v.20), the noise of armies and the chaos of flight (v.29), and the terrified cry of 'daughter Zion' (v.31). In verses 23 to 27, the national and personal tragedies appear as a cosmic catastrophe. God's dark side is the undoing of creation, its return to the chaos, darkness and emptiness that preceded the love of God's creative Spirit (Genesis 1.1-2).

Imagine the prophet spitting out these words. He is addressing not only the people, prophets and priests, but also the officials and the king himself (look back to 4.9-10). These destructive events have not yet happened, so Jeremiah's audience is not yet 'appalled' or 'astounded'. So, Jeremiah must escalate his language, in the desperate hope that they will *listen*. But, from their perspective, all seems well. 'No problem', as people say. Alas, they are self-deceived – and deceive one another. The prophet alone will face and name the terrible reality of God's inevitable judgement in response to his children's rejection.

And yet, is there no hope? A glimmer, at least? Perhaps an ambiguous whisper may be heard in verse 27: 'yet I will not make a full end'.

COLLECT

Almighty God,
whose Son Jesus Christ fasted forty days in the wilderness,
and was tempted as we are, yet without sin:
give us grace to discipline ourselves in obedience to your Spirit;
and, as you know our weakness,
so may we know your power to save;
through Jesus Christ your Son our Lord,
who is alive and reigns with you,
in the unity of the Holy Spirit,
one God, now and for ever.

Psalms **44** *or* **132**, 133
Jeremiah 5.1-19
John 5.19-29

Jeremiah 5.1-19

'... see if you can find one person who acts justly' (v.1)

Verses 1 to 13 read like a lawsuit, with judgement following the formal accusation.

Yahweh suggests a search to try to find a single just person in Jerusalem. No one can be found. This is not unexpected among the poor and unlearned (v.4). But the prophet expects better of the powerful, who are schooled in the faith. But again, no one. So, 'How can I pardon you?', asks the Lord (v.7). 'Shall I not bring retribution on a nation such as this?' (v.9).

The metaphorical wild animals – lion, wolf, leopard – are to be unleashed (v.6); the symbolic devouring fire of God's words will consume the people (v.14). Literally, a foreign nation, 'an enduring ... ancient nation' of warriors will destroy them (vv.15-17).

Is there still a 'yet'? Searching for straws to grasp, we come across two verses that again suggest that the destruction will not be total: that God will not 'make a full end' of the people of Israel (vv.10,18). But their only hope is the hope of exile, far away from the land of God's promises. Once again, as in Egypt before the Exodus, before they knew the grace of God; once again, 'you shall serve strangers in a land that is not yours'.

COLLECT

Heavenly Father,
your Son battled with the powers of darkness,
and grew closer to you in the desert:
help us to use these days to grow in wisdom and prayer
that we may witness to your saving love
in Jesus Christ our Lord.

7

Wednesday 16 March

Jeremiah 5.20-end

'Shall I not punish them for these things?' (v.29)

In both the Old Testament and the New, the theological logic goes: God is like this, God has done and does this; *therefore* you must be and do that. God has brought you out of slavery to this land, *therefore* ... God in Christ has healed and redeemed our lives, *therefore* ...

In verses 22 to 24, it is God's creative power and providential care, expressed in creation, that is presented as the indicative (the statement) that implies the imperative (the exhortation or command) that Israel should acknowledge her creator. But this logic is lost on her. She doesn't fear or tremble. She sees nothing, understands nothing. Stubborn and rebellious to the last, she turns aside. The people's hearts are alienated from their God.

This is not just about a spiritual or religious failing. Verses 25 to 29 present a thoroughgoing *moral* indictment of what has been called the 'practical atheism' of the fat, sleek scoundrels who neglect the claims of the poor and fatherless.

Again, then, the prophet voices God's rhetorical question – 'shall I not bring retribution on a nation such as this?' (v.29). The opportunity for repentance is now past. So, the dreadful question must be posed to Judah: 'what will you do when the end comes?'

COLLECT

Almighty God,
whose Son Jesus Christ fasted forty days in the wilderness,
and was tempted as we are, yet without sin:
give us grace to discipline ourselves in obedience to your Spirit;
and, as you know our weakness,
so may we know your power to save;
through Jesus Christ your Son our Lord,
who is alive and reigns with you,
in the unity of the Holy Spirit,
one God, now and for ever.

Psalms **42**, 43 *or* **143**, 146
Jeremiah 6.9-21
John 6.1-15

Jeremiah 6.9-21

'... because they have not given heed' (v.19)

Jeremiah was called to a ministry of grape-harvesting. It is a 'gleaning' (v.9) that involves searching and picking up the last of the grapes (cf. Jeremiah 49.9). A – literally – fruitless task. There is nothing left, for the vines have been stripped by the nation's faithlessness and her Lord's judgement (Jeremiah 5.10-11).

Yahweh sounds resigned and wounded – but also weary at holding back the anger of his love, the consequence of his people breaking their covenant (v.11). All will suffer its inevitable effects, for all have sinned 'from the least to the greatest' – but the leaders most, by speaking of *shalom* (peace, well-being) instead of warning Israel about its perilous state. Did they feel no shame? (vv.13-15).

We must again imagine the scene in which the prophet speaks out against the status quo and its values, taking on the powerful. We rarely hear such bold critiques, even in safe societies under the rule of impartial law. This is the hard task of prophecy – standing up for something, speaking out for something, preaching before kings the radical word of the Lord.

It is not as though they were ignorant of 'where the good way lies' (v.16) and what the words of God imply. But they have taken no 'heed' (vv.17,19). And so ...

COLLECT

Heavenly Father,
your Son battled with the powers of darkness,
and grew closer to you in the desert:
help us to use these days to grow in wisdom and prayer
that we may witness to your saving love
in Jesus Christ our Lord.

Friday 18 March

Psalms **22** *or* 142, **144**
Jeremiah 6.22-end
John 6.16-27

Jeremiah 6.22-end

'I have made you a tester and a refiner' (v.27)

This prophecy of destruction is unremitting ('terror is on every side', v.25). But the note of sadness is also unquenched ('O my poor people', v.26). Amid the ever-increasing clamour of the invading army, we hear the lamentation of Israel – and that of her prophet, and of her Lord.

And then a personal word to Jeremiah (vv.27-30). Why is the flow of prophecy so often interrupted by such commentaries on the prophet's vocation? Doesn't it smack of self-concerned indulgence? We should recognize that the prophets always felt themselves to be on shaky ground. When you are a prophet, you are often in a minority of one. Everyone else takes a very different view. How could the prophets be sure that they were true, not false prophets? Were they speaking God's word, or just their own thoughts?

The prophet bears a unique, terrible responsibility. He is not just a gleaner of vines. He is also the metallurgist who must assay Israel, to test its character. He is the one authorized to remove its base impurities, so as to separate out the precious metals in the furnace of his speech and acts. And he knows that, should he fail in this vocation to refine Israel, then the Lord will reject his nation as so much dross.

COLLECT

Almighty God,
whose Son Jesus Christ fasted forty days in the wilderness,
and was tempted as we are, yet without sin:
give us grace to discipline ourselves in obedience to your Spirit;
and, as you know our weakness,
so may we know your power to save;
through Jesus Christ your Son our Lord,
who is alive and reigns with you,
in the unity of the Holy Spirit,
one God, now and for ever.

Psalms 25, 147.1-12
Isaiah 11.1-10
Matthew 13.54-end

Saturday 19 March
Joseph of Nazareth

Isaiah 11.1-10

'... and a little child shall lead them' (v.6)

The excuse – should we need one – for breaking our Lenten fast of Jeremiah with this magnificent passage is the reference in v.10 to Jesse, King David's father and the ancestor of the Joseph of the nativity story (see Matthew 1.6,16; Luke 3.23,32). But the shoot from this stump (Isaiah 11.1), which is described so beautifully and powerfully here, is essentially a prophetic expression of future hope for Israel.

In Isaiah's time, Assyria threatened Jerusalem; much later, Babylon would destroy it – and the Davidic monarchy. Nevertheless, Isaiah proclaims God's promise that a new David will arise. And he will be the bearer of God's Spirit, and of God's *vision* (not judging by superficialities, v.3) and *justice* (even for the poor and insignificant, v.4). Especially, he will bear, proclaim and enact God's *peace* (vv.6-9).

This universal peace is imagined as something beyond any peace to which human beings could aspire. It extends even to the natural enmity of predator and prey. This is a most powerful image of Israel's deepest yearning: for a life where none shall 'hurt or destroy'.

Did these words cross Joseph's mind as he looked on Mary's baby, born into an Israel that was still desperately in need of the clear-sighted justice and peace of God?

God our Father,
who from the family of your servant David
raised up Joseph the carpenter
to be the guardian of your incarnate Son
and husband of the Blessed Virgin Mary:
give us grace to follow him
in faithful obedience to your commands;
through Jesus Christ your Son our Lord,
who is alive and reigns with you,
in the unity of the Holy Spirit,
one God, now and for ever.

COLLECT

11

Monday 21 March

Jeremiah 7.21-end

'This is the nation that did not obey' (v.28)

This prose passage begins with harsh words against the sacrificial cultus of Israel (see also Jeremiah 6.20, 7.4). God doesn't care any longer about the niceties of ritual, says Jeremiah. This isn't because the prophet is a Protestant-before-his-time, overturning the ancient patterns of worship. He is rejecting not sacrifice as sacrifice, but any form of worship that is offered with *morally* unclean hands (cf. Micah 6.6-8) and without obedient listening and living (Jeremiah 7.23-24,26,28).

The correct order of things was shown at Sinai. The covenant with Yahweh and its moral stipulations are ratified first before the details of the cultic laws are handed down. What came first must come first. 'Obey my voice, and I will be your God, and you shall be my people; and walk only in the way ...' (v.23).

Hinnom is described in this passage as a place of alien, pagan worship (a 'high place', v.31) and even of human sacrifice, apparently of children. The prophet declares that it will become an open grave for those slaughtered by the invaders. In the New Testament, this valley, where the city's rubbish constantly burned close to the city walls of Jerusalem, is called 'Gehenna' and is used to speak of hell (Mark 9.43-48). Jeremiah is expecting a hell-on-earth.

COLLECT

Almighty God,
you show to those who are in error the light of your truth,
that they may return to the way of righteousness:
grant to all those who are admitted
    into the fellowship of Christ's religion,
that they may reject those things
    that are contrary to their profession,
and follow all such things as are agreeable to the same;
through our Lord Jesus Christ,
who is alive and reigns with you,
in the unity of the Holy Spirit,
one God, now and for ever.

Psalms **50** *or* **5**, 6 (8)
Jeremiah 8.1-15
John 6.52-59

Jeremiah 8.1-15

'Even the stork in the heavens knows its times' (v.7)

The criticism of Israel's rebellious worship continues, with harsh words for those who worshipped the gods of the heavens. In a final indignity – which surely reveals that 'nothing is sacred' (beyond what is truly sacred) – the bones of the honoured dead will be disinterred and scattered 'like dung' (v.2).

The inexplicable and unique nature of the sin of Israel is now underscored. Her continuing disloyalty is represented as an irrational, almost unnatural act. Other peoples would return (v.4), but not they. The rest of creation responds instinctively to the movements of nature, but Israel is unresponsive to God's law. Even the birds migrate when the right season comes round, yet the people of Israel resist to the end the promptings of their lawgiver.

Verse 8 is doubtless the kind of reply that Jeremiah regularly provoked as he preached his message. Their response doesn't matter. 'The wise shall be put to shame' (v.9). God is now pictured as the gleaner of last resort – seeking to harvest any grapes or figs from the withered plants of Israel. But, again, it is a fruitless search (v.13).

The only possibility left is to retreat in the face of the invader. The judgement of God marks their doom. There will be no more harvests.

Almighty God,
by the prayer and discipline of Lent
may we enter into the mystery of Christ's sufferings,
and by following in his Way
come to share in his glory;
through Jesus Christ our Lord.

COLLECT

Wednesday 23 March

Psalm **35** *or* **119.1-32**
Jeremiah 8.18 – 9.11
John 6.60-end

Jeremiah 8.18 – 9.11

'For the hurt of my poor people I am hurt' (8.21)

The roller-coaster experience continues with this heart-rending lament from Jeremiah and the inhabitants of Jerusalem, and perhaps from God. It is an expression of overwhelming grief. 'For the hurt of my poor people I am hurt.' 'Is there no balm in Gilead?' (8.21-22).

But Jeremiah (and Yahweh?) suffer a deep, internal conflict. Their grief for, and love towards, Israel is not in doubt (9.1). But human beings can only stand so much rejection before a desire wells up in their hearts *to leave* (9.2). Does God also feel the pull of these contradictory emotions?

With God it is worse. For all things are in the hands of the Creator God. Why, then, does God not stop these horrors? Jeremiah's answer would be 'because he causes them'. Recoiling at the bluntness of this claim, we might say that, in the providence of the justice of God, they are the inevitable consequence of the rejection of God: 'deceit upon deceit! They refuse to know me ... *Therefore* ...' (9.6-7).

So, verses 9.10 and 11 sit side by side, though uneasily: the cry of compassion, and the harsh reality of the history of the 'chosen people'. And between them lies the hinge on which everything hangs, the mystery of the just *and* loving God.

COLLECT

Almighty God,
you show to those who are in error the light of your truth,
that they may return to the way of righteousness:
grant to all those who are admitted
    into the fellowship of Christ's religion,
that they may reject those things
    that are contrary to their profession,
and follow all such things as are agreeable to the same;
through our Lord Jesus Christ,
who is alive and reigns with you,
in the unity of the Holy Spirit,
one God, now and for ever.

Psalms **34** *or* 14, **15**, 16
Jeremiah 9.12-24
John 7.1-13

Jeremiah 9.12-24

'Do not let the wise boast' (v.23)

At the heart of this passage is another powerful, poetic lament over the ruin of Jerusalem, and the indiscriminate slaughter that causes it. On either side of the dirge sits a prose reflection on wisdom. These passages do not plumb the depths of the wisdom literature of Job and Ecclesiastes, which wrestle with the most intractable issues of life. But they do clearly distinguish a worldly-wise understanding from the insight required to grasp 'the ways of the Lord'. Verses 13 to 15 are blunt. God is now an enemy to his people because they have disobeyed him, which is the logic we have seen elsewhere (see 9.5-9).

Verses 23 to 24 offer us a more profound insight. There is no ground for 'boasting' except in God, and therefore in the knowledge of God and in commitment to the values of God (steadfast love, justice, righteousness). Not in *me*, then, only in God. Paul takes up this theme in 1 Corinthians 1.20-31, where he contrasts the wisdom of the world with the apparent foolishness of choosing the 'low and despised', which is the wisdom of the cross.

Self-satisfaction is anathema to true religion. It has led Israel away from its destiny, and its Lord. The only way forward is through its crucifixion.

Almighty God,
by the prayer and discipline of Lent
may we enter into the mystery of Christ's sufferings,
and by following in his Way
come to share in his glory;
through Jesus Christ our Lord.

COLLECT

15

Friday 25 March
Annunciation of Our Lord
to the Blessed Virgin Mary

Psalms 111, 113
1 Samuel 2.1-10
Romans 5.12-end

Romans 5.12-end

'... by the one man's obedience' (v.19)

To mark the announcement to Mary of her pregnancy and the status of her baby (Luke 1.26-38), we have this profound theological meditation.

Looking back at – rather than forward to – the mission of Christ, Paul sees Jesus as the saviour who cancelled, even reversed, the power of sin that has sucked human beings into enmity with God and the defeat of death. Paul's insight is that the historical Jesus is more than an individual. He is of universal significance: a sort of Adam (Hebrew for 'man'), who was another representative figure. Just as one man changed everything for the worse, so one man has changed everything for the better (vv.18-19).

Both Adam (the 'type of the one who was to come', v.14) and Christ define the character of an age. From the beginning until the coming of Christ, life is distinguished by rebellion, sin and death. But the gracious act ('free gift') of God in Jesus has put things right ('justification', instead of 'condemnation'), leading to the reign of 'righteousness' for others – as grace is made available to 'the many' of humankind.

The young, frightened girl we remember today did not imagine her baby's life in these terms. But she knew something about grace; and she called him 'Jesus', which is shorthand for God's salvation.

COLLECT

We beseech you, O Lord,
pour your grace into our hearts,
that as we have known the incarnation of your Son Jesus Christ
    by the message of an angel,
so by his cross and passion
we may be brought to the glory of his resurrection;
through Jesus Christ your Son our Lord,
who is alive and reigns with you,
in the unity of the Holy Spirit,
one God, now and for ever.

Psalms 3, **25** *or* 20, 21, **23**
Jeremiah 10.17-24
John 7.25-36

Jeremiah 10.17-24

'... not in your anger, or you will bring me to nothing' (v.24)

It is time for Judah to pack its bags and prepare for exile.

The prophet again anticipates the end and speaks of his personal anguish, which must for now stand in for the response of the nation and her own lament. Of course, they will eventually grieve themselves. But will they also recognize their distress as a punishment, as Jeremiah does? And will they, too, acknowledge that they 'must bear it' (v.19)? Will they judge their leaders ('the shepherds', particularly their kings) for stupidly ignoring the will of God?

Most significantly, perhaps, will they join with the prophet in his great prayer of repentance and his plea for a punishment from which they can learn? Israel can only bear a *corrective* punishment that mercifully takes account of human weakness – not the utter destruction of a *punitive* judgement, marked by a strict and just retribution. 'Not in your anger, or you will bring me [us] *to nothing*' (v.24).

Verse 23 might be read in different ways. It may speak of an intrinsic moral weakness in human beings (cf. Jeremiah 17.9), or of their ultimate inability to control their destiny (cf. Jeremiah 18.5-8). On either reading, it is a request for mercy. And the question remains: is God – after all and despite everything – a God of mercy? Will Yahweh stay his hand?

Almighty God,
you show to those who are in error the light of your truth,
that they may return to the way of righteousness:
grant to all those who are admitted
into the fellowship of Christ's religion,
that they may reject those things
that are contrary to their profession,
and follow all such things as are agreeable to the same;
through our Lord Jesus Christ,
who is alive and reigns with you,
in the unity of the Holy Spirit,
one God, now and for ever.

COLLECT

Monday 28 March

Psalms **5**, 7 *or* 27, **30**
Jeremiah 11.1-17
John 7.37-52

Jeremiah 11.1-17

'... he will set fire to it, and its branches will be consumed' (v.16)

When Jeremiah was called to be a prophet by God, he replied: 'Ah! Lord God I am not skilled in speaking ...' Perhaps Jeremiah's response was meant to be an accurate description of how he saw himself, but the fact is he was a remarkable wordsmith, a poet, a man who spoke with a burning energy.

Look carefully at today's passage and you will see some of those poetic skills being put to work. There is a metaphor which runs like a thread through the text: the metaphor of fire.

Jeremiah refers to the children of Israel having been created in a kind of furnace (v.4); then he refers (v.16) to the sound made by an olive tree when it is engulfed in a forest fire; and in verse 17, he rages against the sacrifices made by fire to Baal. In fact, fire is a theme that runs all the way through Jeremiah's work; for example, in chapter 5, verse 14, we read that God said to Jeremiah: 'I am now making my words in your mouth a fire, and this people wood, and the fire shall devour them.'

It's all terrifying stuff. But then, any attempt to speak the truth requires a kind of moral energy that can seem almost overwhelming. How can we be certain that the energy we feel within is really the voice of God? During Lent, we need to take stock of our capacity to deceive ourselves, and pray that we may live with integrity.

COLLECT

Almighty God,
whose most dear Son went not up to joy but first he
    suffered pain,
and entered not into glory before he was crucified:
mercifully grant that we, walking in the way of the cross,
may find it none other than the way of life and peace;
through Jesus Christ your Son our Lord,
who is alive and reigns with you,
in the unity of the Holy Spirit,
one God, now and for ever.

Jeremiah 11.18 – 12.6

'Why does the way of the guilty prosper?' (12.1)

It's a bit disingenuous of Jeremiah, isn't it, to describe himself as a pet lamb being led innocently to the slaughter by his own kith and kin? His fellow villagers in Anathoth cannot have been overjoyed to have this hot-headed prophet in their midst, foretelling chaos and invasion because of their apostasy.

Jeremiah rounds on them and calls on God to wreak vengeance. And God apparently promises that disaster will surely fall on the village. But that isn't enough for Jeremiah; he wants them to be dragged to the slaughter yards.

He sets up a kind of dualism: *I* am an innocent lamb; *they* are sheep who deserve to be killed. It's not very edifying stuff; his sense of betrayal by his own people fuels, perhaps understandably, his anger.

But he then recognizes some of the causes of that anger: 'Why does the way of the guilty prosper? Why do all who are treacherous thrive?' (v.1). His sense of what natural justice demands is in conflict with the evidence of his own eyes. He believes that righteous behaviour should be rewarded, but what seems to happen is the very opposite. He claims that there is a great gulf between what his people outwardly practise and what they inwardly believe. He is looking for an inward conversion, a purifying of the soul so that humankind can become truly integrated. It's a cry that echoes down the corridors of time. And the psychological confusion of his reactions, if we are honest, may have some resonance with how we occasionally feel.

Eternal God,
give us insight
to discern your will for us,
to give up what harms us,
and to seek the perfection we are promised
in Jesus Christ our Lord.

COLLECT

Wednesday 30 March

Jeremiah 13.1-11

'... the loincloth was ruined; it was good for nothing' (v.7)

Sometime Jeremiah lambasts his people with much sound and fury, and then we come across an episode like this in which the parable is quiet, understated and puzzling. This is not a parable for the outsider to ponder, but is one for Jeremiah himself to consider. He is told to buy a loincloth and to bury it in a crevice in some rocks. (There is some dispute about the word *'Perath'*. Some have argued that it suggests a visit to the river Euphrates, known in Hebrew as 'Perath'; others say that it refers to somewhere much closer to Anathoth. The latter seems inherently more likely, because the Euphrates was hundreds of miles away.)

Later, Jeremiah is told by God to go and find the hidden loincloth. He does so and discovers it in tatters. It's a sign that Jeremiah interprets as meaning that God will shred and tear and ruin the people of Judah and Jerusalem. Once they were bound as close to God as a loincloth is bound to a body, but soon they will be torn to shreds.

This passage seems to have two functions. First, it illustrates Jeremiah's growth in understanding. Secondly, it may represent a story remembered about Jeremiah which was seen later to have prophetic immediacy.

Whatever the origin of this strange episode, one thing is clear: Jeremiah believed that the relationship of God with his chosen people was at the point of destruction. He must have felt desperate and intensely alone, for no one seemed to accept what he was saying.

Pray this Lent that any loneliness you feel may be transformed by God into truth-filled courage.

COLLECT

Almighty God,
whose most dear Son went not up to joy but first he
    suffered pain,
and entered not into glory before he was crucified:
mercifully grant that we, walking in the way of the cross,
may find it none other than the way of life and peace;
through Jesus Christ your Son our Lord,
who is alive and reigns with you,
in the unity of the Holy Spirit,
one God, now and for ever.

Psalms **56**, 57 *or* **37***
Jeremiah 14
John 8.31-47

Jeremiah 14

'... we are called by your name; do not forsake us!' (v.9)

There are moments in Jeremiah's life where his desire to speak what he believes to be the truth becomes internalized into prayer. This is one such moment. His love for his people is absolute. Is not the hot anger of truth-telling sometimes born of desire to see improvement because what you love is under threat?

Now he addresses not his people but the Almighty. It is a prayer of heartfelt intensity. Jeremiah yearns for the right relationship between God and his people to be re-established. He sees around him the effects of a drought (is not the description haunting?), and interprets it as a sign of God's absence. He feels as desolate as the parched earth, so he calls to God: 'Yet you, O Lord, are in the midst of us, and we are called by your name; do not forsake us!' (It is the kind of cry that should fill our hearts in Lent.)

The words spiral up into the air. A dialogue ensues, in which God answers that the people have been constantly disobedient, but Jeremiah courageously replies: 'Is it not you, O Lord our God? We set our hope on you ...' (v.22). He begs God to remember the closer-than-covenant relationship which he has with his people. And Jeremiah waits. He can do no more …

Prayer of this kind is based on the belief that, in spite of all things, God remains faithful, true to himself, utterly holy, utterly compassionate.

We meet it in the cry of the man who encountered Jesus and said: 'Lord, I believe, help my unbelief …' (Mark 9.24).

> Eternal God,
> give us insight
> to discern your will for us,
> to give up what harms us,
> and to seek the perfection we are promised
> in Jesus Christ our Lord.

COLLECT

21

Friday I April

Jeremiah 15.10-end

'Woe is me, my mother, that you ever bore me' (v.10)

It is worth remembering that someone, somewhere, once took a papyrus and a stylus and wrote these words that we now read. Perhaps it was Jeremiah himself who did so, which means that we ought to read this text a bit like we might read any other piece of literature. We need to listen to each 'voice', conscious that the 'voice' of God is like that of a character in a play. The words come from the lips of the character, but they began as words in the mind of the playwright.

Jeremiah expresses his sense of personal desolation: 'Woe is me, my mother, that you ever bore me …' (v.10). And he expresses his despair over God: 'Truly, you are to me like a deceitful brook, like waters that fail' (v.18). It is a powerful and courageous lament.

God replies that he will rescue Jeremiah from the clutches of the wicked, from the hands of the ruthless.

Perhaps what we are being given here is a privileged insight into the workings of Jeremiah's soul; the kind of heartfelt conversation that is more often expressed in the solitude of prayer than in public discourse. Whatever its origins may be, and whatever the political situation in which this was written, we should take heart that people before us have felt able to speak to God in prayer with honesty. The more difficult part is then listening for the response, and trying to decide what may be from God and what may be from the deceits of our own nature.

COLLECT

Almighty God,
whose most dear Son went not up to joy but first he
    suffered pain,
and entered not into glory before he was crucified:
mercifully grant that we, walking in the way of the cross,
may find it none other than the way of life and peace;
through Jesus Christ your Son our Lord,
who is alive and reigns with you,
in the unity of the Holy Spirit,
one God, now and for ever.

Psalms **31** *or* 41, **42**, 43
Jeremiah 16.10 – 17.4
John 9.1-17

Jeremiah 16.10 – 17.4

'By your own act you shall lose the heritage that I gave you' (17.4)

There is no comfort for anyone in these verses. God has made his decision, declares Jeremiah. The people who were once his chosen ones have forsaken him. They have run after other gods. They have failed to keep his laws.

The consequences will be unbearable; they will be flung headlong out of the land and be taken to a strange and alien country. Ripped from God and ripped from their homes, they will experience loss of a terrible kind. And, of course, seen in the light of the Exile of 597 BC, this is what happened. The people were taken captive, and by the waters of Babylon sat down and wept.

How far these words of Jeremiah were purely religious prophecies and how far they were an astute reading of the turbulent politics of the Middle East at the time is not for us to know. In any case, for Jeremiah the distinction between politics and religion was not a part of his mental map. All that we can do, centuries later, is to acknowledge that there are times when our understanding of the relationship between God and the facts of history is unclear. The famous hymn, 'God is working His purpose out as year succeeds to year', written by an Old Etonian scholar and teacher, Arthur Campbell Ainger, might have caught the confident mood of late-nineteenth-century expansionist Britain, but in a post-Holocaust Europe, it might raise more questions than it answers.

The relationship between God and the events of our world require the thoughtful and humble attention of us all.

Eternal God,
give us insight
to discern your will for us,
to give up what harms us,
and to seek the perfection we are promised
in Jesus Christ our Lord.

COLLECT

23

Monday 4 April

Psalms **70**, **77** or **44**
Jeremiah 17.5-18
John 9.18-end

Jeremiah 17.5-18

*'Let my persecutors be shamed ...
destroy them with double destruction!' (v.18)*

Proverbs are a good source of wisdom, for they encapsulate the experience of generations of our forebears. In ancient Israel, there was a long tradition of valuing sayings of this kind; you only have to look at the Book of Proverbs to realize that.

In today's passage from Jeremiah, there seem to be a number of sayings that have a proverbial character. For example, 'Blessed are those who trust in the Lord ... They shall be like a tree planted by water, sending out its roots by the stream' (vv.7-8), or 'Like the partridge hatching what it did not lay, so are all who amass wealth unjustly ...' (v.11).

Yet, interspersed with these Wisdom sayings are passages that are clearly meant to reflect the situation in which Jeremiah found himself. He had been warning his people for a long time, and they only responded by saying: 'Where is the word of the Lord? Let it come!' (v.15). In brief, they felt that Jeremiah had been calling 'wolf' for too long.

He was furious at their patronizing response to his message, and he yelled at God: 'Bring on them the day of disaster; destroy them with double destruction!' (v.18).

Is that kind of response to rejection ever justified?

COLLECT

Merciful Lord,
absolve your people from their offences,
that through your bountiful goodness
we may all be delivered from the chains of those sins
which by our frailty we have committed;
grant this, heavenly Father,
for Jesus Christ's sake, our blessed Lord and Saviour,
who is alive and reigns with you,
in the unity of the Holy Spirit,
one God, now and for ever.

Jeremiah 18.1-12

'... like the clay in the potter's hand, so are you in my hand' (v.6)

Almond trees, cauldrons, linen cloths – these were some of the everyday things through which Jeremiah somehow 'saw' God disclosing himself. In today's reading, it is a visit to a potter that enables him to see and hear what God might be saying to him. Watching a potter moulding pots on the wheel, Jeremiah 'sees', as it were, a theological meaning in the action. It is about God's ability to make and remake his people as he wishes. We are clay in his hands.

It is a metaphor that a number of biblical writers had used. Isaiah, for example (Isaiah 29.16), had spoken of the relationship of the clay to the potter, and, centuries later, St Paul used a similar image (Romans 9.20-21). It is unsurprising that everyday trades and crafts should have been the source of metaphors; the same is equally true today. We might say of someone, 'He's a robot', or 'She was programmed to do that'. What it raises is an interesting theological issue. When we use metaphors to talk about God, at what point do we acknowledge that ancient metaphors are no longer adequate? In the twenty-first century in Western Europe, does the metaphor of God as a potter have the power that it must once have had when the craft of pottery was visible on every street corner? When metaphors run out of steam, are we free to abandon them?

Another question: in a period of history when our mental map includes concepts about 'chaos theory' as well as concepts about 'certainty', are we able to talk of God being as free as a potter to make or unmake things at will? The questions are easier to ask than to answer. Perhaps all we can do, especially during Lent, is to try to have the same kind of creativity and integrity that Jeremiah had in how we attempt to speak about God.

Merciful Lord,
you know our struggle to serve you:
when sin spoils our lives
and overshadows our hearts,
come to our aid
and turn us back to you again;
through Jesus Christ our Lord.

COLLECT

25

Wednesday 6 April

Psalms 63, **90** *or* 119.57-80
Jeremiah 18.13-end
John 10.11-21

Jeremiah 18.13-end

'May a cry be heard from their houses ...' (v.22)

Jeremiah was convinced that the Day of Reckoning was coming for his people. He longed for them to change their ways. He spoke passionately about their need to restore their relationship with God, but they refused to listen to him. No matter how powerful his words, no matter how arresting his poetry, they would not respond. They were set in their ways and refused to budge. At least, that is Jeremiah's version of events. It would be interesting to hear the viewpoint of some of those who disagreed with his analysis, but we do not have that available. What we do have is Jeremiah's anxious and fiery message straight, it would seem, from God: 'Like the wind from the east, I will scatter them before the enemy. I will show them my back, not my face, on the day of their calamity' (v.17).

It should have been no surprise to Jeremiah that his message made people so angry that they plotted to get rid of him. He responded with a full-throttle blast of invective: 'Bring raiders on them without warning, and let screaming be heard from their houses ...' (v.22).

It may be understandable as the response of a man who could not get his message across, but it all feels a very long way from the saying of Jesus, 'Blessed are the peacemakers'. But we should not forget that it was out of the long history of God's dealings with his people that Jesus' message arose. Salvation is not achieved overnight.

You might want to consider, this Lent, how strong your relationship is with God, and, if the relationship is fragile, how it can be restored.

COLLECT

Merciful Lord,
absolve your people from their offences,
that through your bountiful goodness
we may all be delivered from the chains of those sins
which by our frailty we have committed;
grant this, heavenly Father,
for Jesus Christ's sake, our blessed Lord and Saviour,
who is alive and reigns with you,
in the unity of the Holy Spirit,
one God, now and for ever.

Psalms 53, **86** *or* 56, **57** (63*)
Jeremiah 19.1-13
John 10.22-end

Jeremiah 19.1-13

*'So will I break this people and this city,
as one breaks a potter's vessel' (v.11)*

There are occasions in the Bible when the actual text seems a bit confused, as though an editor has sewn two sections together and has placed them in the wrong position. This may be the case in today's reading. If you read verses 1-2 and then jump straight to verse 10, the story makes sense. In the first verses, the people addressed are the elders and the priests. The second section, beginning at verse 3, is addressed not to the elders and priests but to the princes and the people of Jerusalem. It could be that the editor has put the two stories together because they both refer to a potter and his earthenware jars.

Whatever the cause of the textual confusion might be, the message is clear. Jeremiah proclaims in word and symbolic action that terrible trouble lies very close at hand. God is about to judge his people. And why? Because the people have been worshipping other gods and have been involved in the sacrificial killing of innocent children. So, Jeremiah smashes the earthenware pot and says that, just as the jar lies scattered and cannot be remade, so will their dead bodies be.

It is a chilling and awful proclamation, which was even more terrifying for those who believed that symbolic actions actually brought about the things that they foretold.

Merciful Lord,
you know our struggle to serve you:
when sin spoils our lives
and overshadows our hearts,
come to our aid
and turn us back to you again;
through Jesus Christ our Lord.

COLLECT

Psalms **102** *or* **51**, 54
Jeremiah 19.14 – 20.6
John 11.1-16

Jeremiah 19.14 – 20.6

'... a terror to yourself and to all your friends' (20.4)

The tension created by Jeremiah's tough prophecies was bound to break sooner or later. In today's passage, we come to that moment.

Jeremiah's smashing of the earthenware pot had taken place at or very near Topheth, the place in the valley of Hinnom, where people had been sacrificing their children by burning them alive in honour of the god Moloch. Having berated the people for such an appalling practice, Jeremiah now re-enters Jerusalem. He goes to the centre of power, the temple, and there he continues his tirade, saying that God will bring destruction on all.

He was arrested by a priest called Passhur and was placed overnight in the stocks. The ordeal did nothing to cool Jeremiah's religious convictions. In the morning, he railed against Passhur, giving him a new name that meant 'fear/terror on every side', or 'terror let loose', and said that Passhur would be carried into captivity by the approaching enemy.

There is an underlying irony in this story. Jeremiah's name means 'Yahweh exalts'. And here he is, a man from an outlying village, whose very name should have been a warning to those who refused to listen, clashing with one of the most powerful priests in Jerusalem, one whose main function should have been to give glory to God through the sacrificial system at the temple. It's the outsider who would seem to be closer to God than the insider, and the outsider who says that everything in the centre will be demolished by God. It is radical in the extreme.

COLLECT

Merciful Lord,
absolve your people from their offences,
that through your bountiful goodness
we may all be delivered from the chains of those sins
which by our frailty we have committed;
grant this, heavenly Father,
for Jesus Christ's sake, our blessed Lord and Saviour,
who is alive and reigns with you,
in the unity of the Holy Spirit,
one God, now and for ever.

Psalms **32** *or* **68**
Jeremiah 20.7-end
John 11.17-27

Jeremiah 20.7-end

'Why did I come forth from the womb to ... spend my days in shame?' (v.18)

And then, having challenged one of the most powerful men of his city, and having withstood the loneliness and humiliation of the stocks, Jeremiah's confidence suddenly deserts him.

It is a moment of intense poignancy. Nothing we have read of Jeremiah's courage and resilient determination up to now can quite prepare us for the shock of this haunting passage. This is a soul in the very depths of despair: 'You have duped me, Lord, and I have been your dupe ...' God is nowhere to be found. He is appallingly absent. It is a cry of dereliction from the depths of Jeremiah's being. For a moment, we are left to wonder what will become of this audacious but now broken man.

His courage wells up. He recalls that trying not to speak of the things of God was impossible; it was like a fire burning in his heart. And, as soon as he remembers this inner reality, he calls out, 'But the Lord is with me like a dread warrior' (v.11), and soon he is singing out the praises of God, only to succumb almost immediately to spiritual anguish: 'Cursed be the day on which I was born!' (v.14).

There are some biblical passages where the very core of our humanity is exposed, our noblest and our most fragile self has nowhere left to hide. We are alone.

Words stop. All we can do is to wait in that place where certainty and uncertainty are one, and in our desolation call upon God for mercy.

Lent provides us with an opportunity to wait upon the merciful kindness of the Lord.

Merciful Lord,
you know our struggle to serve you:
when sin spoils our lives
and overshadows our hearts,
come to our aid
and turn us back to you again;
through Jesus Christ our Lord.

COLLECT

29

Monday 11 April

Jeremiah 21.1-10

'I am setting before you the way of life and the way of death' (v.8)

The historical context of this passage is clear. It is the year 588 BC. Jerusalem is being blockaded by the Babylonians. In terms of Middle Eastern politics, the rulers of Judah, prior to this, had tried to arrange an alliance with the Egyptians against the rising might of Babylon, but it was all to no avail. The Babylonian forces were now massing at the approaches to Jerusalem. The King of Judah, Zedekiah, sends a message to Jeremiah asking him to intercede with God for a miracle. Jeremiah's reaction is swift, brutal and uncompromising: 'Thus says the Lord, the God of Israel ... I myself will fight against you ... in anger, in fury, and in great wrath' (vv.3,5).

Jeremiah had spoken. But he did offer a piece of realpolitik advice: surrender to the besieging armies and you might survive; stay in the city and you will all be slaughtered.

It is not difficult to imagine the flurry of anxious consultations that must have gone on among the political leaders in Jerusalem once Jeremiah's advice was received: should they heed his warnings or not? It was hawks versus doves.

And what was Jeremiah thinking? For one who loved his country and his people passionately, he must have been heartbroken. His conscience would not allow him to compromise what he said, but where was God's plan in all of this?

COLLECT

Most merciful God,
who by the death and resurrection of your Son Jesus Christ
delivered and saved the world:
grant that by faith in him who suffered on the cross
we may triumph in the power of his victory;
through Jesus Christ your Son our Lord,
who is alive and reigns with you,
in the unity of the Holy Spirit,
one God, now and for ever.

Psalms **35**, 123 *or* **73**
Jeremiah 22.1-5,13-19
John 11.45-end

Jeremiah 22.1-5,13-19

'... obey this word' (v.4)

One of the difficulties in reading the Book of Jeremiah is that it is does not always follow a strict historical sequence. In yesterday's reading, we were looking at events in the year 588 BC; in today's reading, we seem to be many years earlier in the reign of Jehoiakim. He was the vassal king of Judah who had been put in place by Pharaoh Neko II in 608 BC. He played a devious political hand and switched allegiance to the Babylonians for three years, but then switched back to the Egyptians. It was not a clever move.

Meanwhile, he was assailed in Jerusalem by the uncompromising voice of Jeremiah, who forcefully reminded him of his religious and moral obligations, and of the consequences of failure to obey God: 'I shall consecrate an armed host to fight against you, a destructive horde ...'

In 599 BC, Nebuchadnezzar II of Babylon laid siege to Jerusalem. In 598 BC, Jehoiakim died, and within three months Jerusalem fell. Many of the leading citizens were exiled to Babylon, and the Babylonians installed a new vassal king in Jerusalem, Zedekiah. (We met him in yesterday's reading.)

No matter whether the king of Judah was a vassal of Egypt or of Babylon, Jeremiah did not waver. His message was that it was God who had to be obeyed, not man, and obeyed completely. Nothing less would do. That was Israel's solemn religious and moral duty.

Consider this Lent whether you feel you serve God obediently.

Gracious Father,
you gave up your Son
out of love for the world:
lead us to ponder the mysteries of his passion,
that we may know eternal peace
through the shedding of our Saviour's blood,
Jesus Christ our Lord.

COLLECT

Wednesday 13 April

Psalms **55**, 124 *or* **77**
Jeremiah 22.20 – 23.8
John 12.1-11

Jeremiah 22.20 – 23.8

'I will raise up for David a righteous Branch' (23.5)

If only the editors of the Book of Jeremiah had had a stronger sense of chronology …

In today's readings (22.20-27), we have a prophecy about a future catastrophe when the people and their rulers will be taken captive; but this is immediately followed by a saying which implies that the exile has already begun. It does not make for easy reading.

The passage that follows, however, brings a rapid change of mood. We are introduced to a powerful lament ('O land, land, land ...', 22.29), which takes us into Jeremiah's heart. He can see that the shepherds of Israel have not watched over God's own flock. They have failed to fulfil their God-given duty. And the result is a tragedy.

Nevertheless, even in such harrowing times, Jeremiah proclaims that God will one day make a righteous branch spring from David's line, a king who will 'deal wisely, and shall execute justice and righteousness in the land' (23.5). He foretells that the exile will end and that the people will be able to return to their own soil. In the midst of despair, he sees God-born hope.

The longing for a righteous king eventually fed into Jewish messianic expectations, and therefore into the life of Christ. Bring to mind Mary's song: 'He has come to the help of Israel his servant, as he promised to our forefathers; he has not forgotten to show mercy to Abraham and his children's children for ever.'

COLLECT

Most merciful God,
who by the death and resurrection of your Son Jesus Christ
delivered and saved the world:
grant that by faith in him who suffered on the cross
we may triumph in the power of his victory;
through Jesus Christ your Son our Lord,
who is alive and reigns with you,
in the unity of the Holy Spirit,
one God, now and for ever.

Psalms **40**, 125 *or* **78.1-39***
Jeremiah 23.9-32
John 12.12-19

Jeremiah 23.9-32

'... a hammer that breaks a rock in pieces' (v.29)

The verses in the first part of today's reading (vv.9-15) probably come from the earlier part of Jeremiah's life. There is nothing in them to suggest that the words were spoken close to the catastrophe of the Exile. But the verses that follow (vv.16-24) might be much closer in time to that disaster.

Nevertheless, the entire passage has a strong and critical message: there are bad prophets and there are faithful, good prophets. The bad prophets are those who speak wispy words of easy comfort. But prophets who stand close to the counsel of God and speak the truth are the ones who should be heard. The truth from God has a terrifying force: 'Is not my word like fire, says the Lord, and like a hammer that breaks a rock in pieces?'

At the heart of Jeremiah's book is the belief that God is utterly holy, a God of purity, a God of justice, a fearsome God; one who demands the highest standards of righteous behaviour from his people.

It is an idea that also finds a place in the New Testament. In the Epistle to the Hebrews occurs this: 'Therefore, since we are receiving a kingdom that cannot be shaken, let us give thanks, by which we offer to God an acceptable worship with reverence and awe; for indeed our God is a consuming fire' (Hebrews 12.28-29). They are the kind of words that Jeremiah might have written himself.

Gracious Father,
you gave up your Son
out of love for the world:
lead us to ponder the mysteries of his passion,
that we may know eternal peace
through the shedding of our Saviour's blood,
Jesus Christ our Lord.

COLLECT

33

Friday 15 April

Psalms **22**, 126 *or* **55**
Jeremiah 24
John 12.20-36a

Jeremiah 24

'... they shall be my people' (v.7)

If only we knew when this chapter was written ...

If it is an account of a vision of Jeremiah after the leaders had been sent into exile, we should read it as a remarkable and courageous statement – a statement suggesting that all those who remained in Jerusalem were dross, and those who had been exiled were the true people of God. It is not at all what we would expect Jeremiah to say after all the harsh things he had written about the leaders previously.

However, if this passage was written once the exiles had returned from Babylon to Jerusalem in 538 BC (and there are scholars who regard parts of the Book of Jeremiah as dating from this time), then we might read it as a piece of political propaganda created by the returning exiles, staking their claim to be the true Israel.

It really is not possible at this distance in time to distinguish with certainty between these two interpretations of the passage. Perhaps, in such circumstances, we ought to opt more strongly for the first interpretation, that is, that this account really does pre-date the exile. In that case, what we are reading is Jeremiah's conviction that God would not allow the Exile to prevent reconciliation with himself: 'they shall be my people and I will be their God' (v.7).

Can anything, as St Paul asked, ever separate us from God's love? Allow yourself this Lent to accept that God's love for you is unshakeable.

COLLECT

Most merciful God,
who by the death and resurrection of your Son Jesus Christ
delivered and saved the world:
grant that by faith in him who suffered on the cross
we may triumph in the power of his victory;
through Jesus Christ your Son our Lord,
who is alive and reigns with you,
in the unity of the Holy Spirit,
one God, now and for ever.

Jeremiah 25.1-14

'I have spoken persistently to you, but you have not listened' (v.3)

This passage begins with a very precise date: the fourth year of Jehoiakim, the king of Judah. We can say with reasonable certainty that this was 604 BC. In the previous year, 605 BC, there had been a remarkably significant battle between the Babylonians on the one side and a combined Assyrian/Egyptian force on the other. The Babylonians won, and this marked the end of Assyrian hegemony in that part of the Middle East. A new balance of power came into being. Jehoiakim, king of Judah, therefore, who had been installed as a vassal king of Judah by the Egyptians, now changed sides and started to pay tribute to the Babylonians.

Meanwhile, Jeremiah used the moment of huge political change to summarize his previous 23 years of public prophecies. His message was that he had been bringing to his people the Word of the Lord, but they had refused to listen. They had continued to worship other gods; they had refused to pay proper allegiance to Yahweh. The result, he said, would be a terrible judgement; the Babylonians would be used by God to fulfil his will: 'I will bring them against this land and its inhabitants ... I will utterly destroy them' (v.9). But, the prophecy went on, eventually the Babylonians would be punished by God.

Jeremiah saw in the struggle for territorial power in the Middle East the workings of God. He believed that he was being used by God to speak the revelation of this truth to his generation. It was a tough assignment – but the discernment of truth, and the speaking of truth, in any age, cannot be achieved without great courage and tenacity, can it?

Gracious Father,
you gave up your Son
out of love for the world:
lead us to ponder the mysteries of his passion,
that we may know eternal peace
through the shedding of our Saviour's blood,
Jesus Christ our Lord.

COLLECT

Monday 18 April

Monday of Holy Week

Luke 22.1-23

*'Now the festival of Unleavened Bread, which is called the Passover,
was near' (v. 1)*

The setting of the Last Supper at the time of the Passover is significant.
We are reminded of the great act of deliverance by which God rescued
his people at the time of the Exodus. Luke has already spoken of Jesus
accomplishing his Exodus in Jerusalem in the conversation with Moses
and Elijah at the transfiguration (Luke 9.30).

As they gather for the meal, Jesus tells the disciples that this Passover,
which he has been longing to share with them, will be the last
Passover he will take part in until the kingdom of God comes. Then he
takes bread and wine, as he would normally do as the host, and invests
them with new meaning. When they share bread in future, it will be
his body, his way of being present with them, and the wine will be his
blood, the sign of the new covenant that will be inaugurated through
his suffering.

All this is enacted against the background of the forces of evil
mounting their attack on Jesus, through the religious leaders trying to
find a way to get rid of him, and through Judas who provides them
with the means to achieve their end. Jesus warns his disciples of
impending betrayal. But they are unable to grasp his meaning, and
wonder whom he means.

COLLECT

Almighty and everlasting God,
who in your tender love towards the human race
   sent your Son our Saviour Jesus Christ
to take upon him our flesh
and to suffer death upon the cross:
grant that we may follow the example of his patience and
   humility,
and also be made partakers of his resurrection;
through Jesus Christ your Son our Lord,
who is alive and reigns with you,
in the unity of the Holy Spirit,
one God, now and for ever.

Psalm 27
Lamentations 3.1-18
Luke 22.[24-38] 39-53

Luke 22.[24-38] 39-53

'… not my will but yours be done' (v.42)

Just when Jesus could have done with their support, the disciples get into an argument about which of them is the greatest, and Jesus has to remind them about his servant model of service. Peter (addressed as Simon, indicating that he is about to revert to his status before he was called Peter 'the rock') is warned that he will deny knowing Jesus, despite his protestations of loyalty. Do we get distracted like the disciples by trivial arguments, or refuse to face our own fragility?

Then comes the final choice for Jesus. He knows that God's will is that evil must be defeated, and that the only way to break its power is to face it, absorb it and not hit back. Humanly speaking, he can't bear the thought of what lies ahead: 'Father, if you are willing, remove this cup from me' (v.42). But he had come to be the agent of God's will, and in agony he makes his decision, and says: 'not my will but yours be done'. His decision is given God's seal of acceptance through the ministry of the angel who comes to strengthen him.

What follows is inevitable once he has made his choice. He is betrayed by a kiss, and it seems that darkness has won.

True and humble king,
hailed by the crowd as Messiah:
grant us the faith to know you and love you,
that we may be found beside you
on the way of the cross,
which is the path of glory.

COLLECT

37

Wednesday 20 April

Wednesday of Holy Week

Psalm 102 [or 102.1-18]
Jeremiah 11.18-20
Luke 22.54-end

Luke 22.54-end

'The Lord turned and looked at Peter' (v.61)

Peter has repeatedly said that he will not desert Jesus, in spite of all the warnings Jesus has given him. He does at least follow, albeit at a distance, as far as the courtyard of the high priest's house where Jesus had been taken. Here the challenge comes, and three times Peter denies any link with Jesus. Hardly has the third denial passed his lips than the cock crows. And the Lord turns and looks at Peter.

That look must have been one of compassion, rather than an 'I told you so' look. If it had been the latter, Peter would probably have got defensive. ('I know I said I would never forsake you, but I didn't think you'd go this far – I've got a wife and family to think of.') But that wasn't his response. Perhaps Peter remembered at that moment what Jesus had said earlier: 'Simon, Simon, listen! Satan has demanded to sift all of you like wheat, but I have prayed for you ['you' in the singular here] that your own faith may not fail; and you, when once you have turned back, strengthen your brothers' (Luke 22.31-32). Realizing that Jesus understood was enough to move him to tears.

Isn't it Jesus' compassion that moves us to repentance too?

COLLECT

Almighty and everlasting God,
who in your tender love towards the human race
    sent your Son our Saviour Jesus Christ
to take upon him our flesh
and to suffer death upon the cross:
grant that we may follow the example of his patience and
    humility,
and also be made partakers of his resurrection;
through Jesus Christ your Son our Lord,
who is alive and reigns with you,
in the unity of the Holy Spirit,
one God, now and for ever.

Psalms 42, 43
Leviticus 16.2-24
Luke 23.1-25

Luke 23.1-25

'I have found in him no ground for the sentence of death' (v.22)

The one thing Pilate couldn't stand was a shouting mob. When he took up his post in Jerusalem, he had marched into the city with Roman standards flying, and the people had rioted in protest. Pilate gave in, and the Roman symbols were removed. But the people had discovered his weak spot. Now, when they shouted for Jesus' death, his blood ran cold. He couldn't risk an uprising – it would be more than his job was worth.

He looked for loopholes. The man came from Galilee, which was not his responsibility, so he sent Jesus to Herod, who wanted to meet him anyway. But Herod, although he appreciated the friendly gesture by someone he had regarded as an enemy, failed to take responsibility, and Jesus came back to Pilate.

Pilate did try to get Jesus released, but the mob's shouting continued, and their voices prevailed. So, Jesus was condemned to death.

We are used to talking about sins of omission or commission. But there is a third category too: that of *permission*, the things we allow to happen because we haven't got the will or the courage to challenge them.

Which category do our sins fall into on the whole?

True and humble king,
hailed by the crowd as Messiah:
grant us the faith to know you and love you,
that we may be found beside you
on the way of the cross,
which is the path of glory.

COLLECT

39

Friday 22 April

Good Friday

Psalm 69
Genesis 22.1-18
John 19.38-end *or* Hebrews 10.1-10

Hebrews 10.1-10

'... we have been sanctified ... once for all' (v.10)

'Once, only once, and once for all
His precious life he gave;
Before the cross our spirits fall,
And own it strong to save.'

The words of William Bright's hymn develop the thoughts of the writer of the Letter to the Hebrews. The author refers back to the instructions in Leviticus 16 for the offering of sacrifice in atonement for sin. The elaborate ritual for the cleansing of God's people under the terms of the old covenant had to be repeated each year. More than one Old Testament writer, as time passed, had pointed out that God was not interested in sacrificial offerings that meant nothing if they were not accompanied by a change of heart: Psalm 40.6-8; Amos 5.21-24.

Jesus said the same, as the writer to the Hebrews says: 'in burnt-offerings and sin-offerings you have taken no pleasure' (v.6). By his self-offering, Jesus has inaugurated the new covenant sealed with his blood, and the old rituals can be dispensed with. Now everyone has the opportunity of being set free by God's forgiveness.

Small wonder, then, that when we gather for worship on this day and contemplate the cross, we often say:

'We adore you O Christ and we bless you,
Because by your cross and passion you have redeemed the world.'

COLLECT

Almighty Father,
look with mercy on this your family
for which our Lord Jesus Christ was content to be betrayed
    and given up into the hands of sinners
    and to suffer death upon the cross;
who is alive and glorified with you and the Holy Spirit,
one God, now and for ever.

Psalm 142
Hosea 6.1-6
John 2.18-22

John 2.18-22

'Destroy this temple, and in three days I will raise it up' (v.19)

Unlike the other Gospel-writers, John placed what we call the cleansing of the temple at the beginning of Jesus' ministry. Jesus' action understandably raised questions about his authority for acting in such a cavalier fashion. Jesus told his questioners: 'Destroy this temple, and in three days I will raise it up.' The Jews didn't understand – it had taken them 46 years to build the temple, so how could anyone rebuild it in three days? With hindsight, after the resurrection, his disciples remembered what he had said, and understood that he was referring to the temple of his own body, the dwelling place of God, and that he had indeed been raised on the third day.

The temple, because of the way the religious leaders had allowed it to become corrupted into a commercial enterprise rather than a place of prayer, had ceased to fulfil its proper function. Jesus would provide in himself the place where people could meet God. Paul would later develop the idea of each believer being the dwelling place of God (1 Corinthians 3.16-17, 6.19).

Are we fit for purpose as temples of God? Or do we need cleansing too?

COLLECT

Grant, Lord,
that we who are baptized into the death
of your Son our Saviour Jesus Christ
may continually put to death our evil desires
and be buried with him;
and that through the grave and gate of death
we may pass to our joyful resurrection;
through his merits,
who died and was buried and rose again for us,
your Son Jesus Christ our Lord.